THIS BOOK BELONGS TO...

_____

WEEK 1

WEEK 2

She Believed She Could
So She Did

WEEK 3

WEEK 4

_____

_____

_____

_____

_____

_____

_____

_____

_____

_____

_____

_____

_____

_____

_____

You've Got This

WEEK 5

WEEK 6

No Matter How You Feel...
Get up, Dress up, Show up &
Never Give Up

WEEK 7

WEEK 8

_Don't Let Anything
Dull your Sparkle_

WEEK 9

WEEK 10

"Nothing is Impossible,
the word itself says,
I'm Possible!"
Audrey Hepburn

WEEK 11

WEEK 12

Leave a Little Sparkle
Wherever You Go

WEEK 13

WEEK 14

Positiveness
is your Superpower

WEEK 15

WEEK 16

You don't know how
STRONG you are until
You have to Be

WEEK 17

WEEK 18

_____

_____

_____

_____

_____

_____

_____

_____

_____

_____

_____

_____

_____

_____

_____

"Hardships often prepare
ordinary people for an
extraordinary destiny" C.S. Lewis

WEEK 19

WEEK 20

Don't look back
you are not going
that way

WEEK 21

WEEK 22

You Never Met a
Strong Person
with an Easy Past

WEEK 23

WEEK 24

"Never
Ever Ever Ever Ever
Give up" Winston Churchill

WEEK 25

WEEK 26

Believe in Miracles

WEEK 27

WEEK 28

_____

_____

_____

_____

_____

_____

_____

_____

_____

_____

_____

_____

_____

_____

_____

_____

_____

_____

Always Remember...
You are Braver than you think,
Stronger than you seem, Loved More
than you Know

WEEK 29

WEEK 30

_____

_____

_____

_____

_____

_____

_____

_____

_____

_____

_____

_____

_____

"Women are like Tea Bags
You Never Know how Strong they
are until they are in Hot Water"
Eleanor Roosevelt

WEEK 31

WEEK 32

_____

_____

_____

_____

_____

_____

_____

_____

_____

_____

_____

_____

_____

_____

_____

_____

_____

_____

_____

_____

_____

_____

*My Courage is
Stronger than my Fear*

WEEK 33

WEEK 34

You Have Been Assigned
this Mountain to show
Others that it can be Moved

WEEK 35

WEEK 36

She stood in the storm & when the wind did not
blow her away,
she adjusted her sails

WEEK 37

WEEK 38

_____

_____

_____

_____

_____

_____

_____

_____

_____

_____

_____

_____

_____

_____

_____

"Believe you can and you're halfway there."

Theodore Roosevelt

WEEK 39

WEEK 40

_Sometimes you are
forced to go through
things and not around them_

WEEK 41

WEEK 42

When you come to the end of
your rope, tie a knot & hang on

WEEK 43

WEEK 44

Some Days You have to Create
Your Own Sunshine

WEEK 45

WEEK 46

Begin Each Day with
a Grateful Heart

WEEK 47

WEEK 48

One Small Positive Thought in the Morning Can Change the Whole Day

WEEK 49

WEEK 50

_____

_____

_____

_____

_____

_____

_____

_____

_____

_____

_____

_____

_____

_____

_____

_____

Laughter is the Best Medicine, and
the next Best Thing to a Cure

WEEK 51

WEEK 52

Everything you can Image, Is Real.
Pablo Picasso